Negotiation from
A to Z

By

Nicole Davidson

Nicole Davidson

Negotiation from A to Z

First published by GrowingBeyond Pty Ltd 2020

Copyright © 2020 by Nicole Davidson

Nicole Davidson has no responsibility for the persistence or accuracy of URLs for external or third-party Internet Websites referred to in this publication and does not guarantee that any content on such Websites is, or will remain, accurate or appropriate.

First edition

This book was professionally typeset on Reedsy

Find out more at reedsy.com

This book is dedicated to my husband and children who always give me plenty of opportunity to negotiate and let me test out my new theories on them without complaint (or at least not too much!)

PREFACE

I have a confession to make - I am a total negotiation nerd! After many years in various commercial roles, from lawyer to investment banker to insolvency practitioner to learning & development manager it was when I moved to a role with a negotiation consultancy that I found my passion. For the last eight years, I have been focused on understanding the theory behind negotiations and connecting that with my varied experiences in my professional life.

Two years ago, I set out a write a series of tips for people to assist them in getting more from their negotiations. This book is the culmination of this work. It does not seek to be a comprehensive overview of negotiation. What it does seek to be is a series of bite-sized chunks of practical ideas which you can quickly and easily implement to improve your negotiations.

I hope you find the tips useful. If these whet your appetite to build your negotiation skills to the next level, get in touch with me via www.nicoledavidsonnegotiation.com.au to learn how I can help.

Best wishes

Nicole

CONTENTS

A IS FOR ALTERNATIVES

———————•-•● ● ●•-•———————

It might seem a little strange to start an A to Z of negotiation with a discussion of alternatives. This is because when we talk about alternatives, we are looking at what happens if we don't reach agreement in the negotiation. For many people, this equates to the negotiation being a failure.

Understanding our alternatives clearly, helps us to redefine what success means in a negotiation perspective. Alternatives consider plan B. What other actions are available to us if we don't do a deal with our negotiation counterpart. If we can meet our interests better by abandoning the negotiation, failing to reach agreement does not make the negotiation unsuccessful (at least from our perspective!).

Unfortunately, once we have invested time, money and emotion in a negotiation, it's easy to lose sight of the alternatives. We may end up agreeing to something that was in fact worse than our alternative. Now that's an unsuccessful negotiation!

Raising your alternatives in a negotiation can be a tricky business. It can easily come across as a threat, significantly impacting the relationship. Consider the infamous Tim Tam negotiation[1] where Campbells Arnotts threatened to stop supply of Tim Tams to Coles if Coles didn't agree to a price rise. The resulting publicity didn't do any good to either party.

A study by Pinkley[2] tells us however, that there can be a real benefit in communicating your alternative to your counterparty when your alternative is strong. The subjects who disclosed their alternatives had more positive outcomes than those that didn't. Finding a way to subtly make the new buyer aware of the first offer is likely to mean that their initial offer is higher than it might otherwise have been.

A further study showed that disclosure of a strong alternative is likely to lead the other party to make a more favourable opening offer. As a negotiation, statistically, is likely to end around the mid-point of the two opening offers, improving the opening offer has a positive effect on the outcome.

So, next time you are preparing to negotiate, don't forget to think about what avenues are open to you if you can't reach agreement.

B IS FOR BIAS

It often strikes me that if computers were to negotiate, they would do a far more efficient job than we do as humans. Not only are computers devoid of the emotion that affects human decision making (and I'm not suggesting that emotion doesn't play an important role in negotiation!) but they are not subject to the imperfections of human data processing.

Those imperfections are technically known as cognitive biases. These biases lead us to make systematic errors when we process information. The difficulty we have is that these biases are so ingrained that it is difficult to avoid them even if you are aware that they exist. In one study[3], even though participants were told about the biases, they are unable to counteract the impacts.

There are approximately 175 of these biases, some of which I will be covering in future posts. A couple of the big ones to watch out for in your negotiations are:

- **Reactive devaluation** - This is where the very fact that a proposal comes from our negotiating counterparty leads us to devalue the proposal without full consideration. This impact is exacerbated where the proposal comes from someone we don't like or trust.

- **Information availability** – we are more influenced by information that is presented in vivid, colourful or attention-getting ways and will believe information that is presented clearly more readily than information that is confusing or overly detailed.

- **Commitment escalation** – once we have commenced a negotiation, we are likely to continue down the negotiation path, even where new information comes to hand that changes the likelihood of a positive outcome.

I encountered a classic example of commitment escalation recently with a client. Kieran headed a national sales team. His team had been in negotiations with a government department for a large contract for over 12 months. When we analysed the parties' interests and alternatives it became clear that the chances of getting to a successful outcome were low. In fact, Kieran stood a much better chance of getting a deal signed by focusing on other clients. He told me that he'd had doubts about the deal for some time but was reluctant to let it go as he'd promised at his job interview that he'd bring in this new client.

So, while we don't want to lose our humanity and become computer negotiators, try to keep in mind the biases which may impact you and, where the stakes are high, seek an outside opinion to challenge your own perspectives.

C IS FOR CONCESSIONS

In a negotiation, a concession is any offer made that is more favourable to the other party than the previous offer. Where the parties expect distributive bargaining, or haggling, there are likely to be a series of concessions made during the negotiation until agreement is reached. That the number reached is likely to be close to the midpoint of the two opening offers.

To improve your negotiations, it is important to understand how to manage the reciprocity, size and timing of concessions.

Reciprocity of concessions

I remember early in my career, attending a negotiation course where I was told that "one should never grant a concession without getting a concession in return". While I'm not a believer of black and white statements like this one, there is some sense in seeking mutual concessions rather than making unilateral concessions. The word "if" is a powerful tool for making this happen.

Take for example a situation where you are negotiating for a consulting contract. The client has asked you to reduce your fee by $300 a day. Rather than simply making this unilateral concession, you may choose to make it a mutual concession by suggesting "I could agree to a reduction of the daily rate if you were to agree to weekly rather than monthly billing."

Size of concessions

Obviously, it is possible to make small or large concessions. It is important to be careful when making concessions however as they may have the opposite effect to what you intend.

Take for example the salesperson who each time they drop the price dropped by more than the customer increases their price. Research[4] shows us that this will actually lead to reduced client satisfaction.

In other research, it was shown that a strategy of starting a negotiation with tough stance of few early concessions and then switching to larger concessions later in the negotiation was more effective than starting with large concessions or sticking only with small concessions[5]. It seems that this strategy works as it creates a contrast for the other side who feels a sense of relief once more generous concessions start being made. It gives the other party a sense of "winning" in the negotiation.

Timing of concessions

It is important not to make concessions too early in the negotiation. Kwon and Weingart[6] showed that a buyer is more satisfied in a negotiation when the seller makes gradual concessions. Sellers who made immediate concessions had the most negative reaction from the buyers.

A final note on concessions

If you are making a concession during your negotiation, make sure the other party knows that you have made it. By making the concession explicit, you are likely to trigger a sense of reciprocity in the other party. They are then more likely to make a concession in return. When sharing your concession, make sure you make it clear to the other party what the cost is to you if you want as well is the benefit to them.

D IS FOR DISTRIBUTIVE BARGAINING

———————•••●●●•••———————

While we may negotiate over hundreds of different types of outcomes, there are two main methods of negotiation - distributive or integrative (or interest-based) negotiation.

Distributive negotiation is based on the idea that there is a fixed resource (often money). After the negotiation concludes, one party will have more of the resource and the other party will have less. Distributive negotiation generally is a one-dimensional process.

On the other hand, integrative negotiation tries to expand the amount of resources that can be brought to the equation. Rather than simply looking at one resource it may consider a range of other factors. This is often described as "growing the pie" so that there are more resources to be shared by both parties.

Take for example, a negotiation to buy a car. In a purely distributive negotiation, there are two key questions. How much is the buyer willing to pay and how much is the seller willing to accept. Obviously, the buyer wants to pay as little as possible and the seller to receive as much as possible. Assume that the seller opens the bidding with a price of

$25,000. The buyer may counter with an offer of $20,000. We would expect to see some haggling and various concessions until the parties reach agreement. We know from research that generally, a distributive negotiation will end up somewhere around the midpoint of the two initial offers. Here we would expect to see a deal done at around $22,500.

Compare that to an integrative approach. Here, before discussing price the parties will find out more about each other's needs. The buyer may ask the seller why they are selling the car. They learn that the seller is in fact about to move overseas in six weeks' time. They are not in a hurry to sell the car but wanted to start the process early so they would not be pressured into accepting a low price. In fact, they would really prefer not to sell the car just yet as they will need it over the next six weeks and may need to hire a car if they to sell early.

The seller asks the buyer about how they come to be interested in the car. The buyer discloses that this is their first car. They are about to move into a new apartment in a months' time. Where they are living at the moment there is no parking available and they would need to be parking the car at their parents' house some distance away until they move.

The parties quickly identify that there is value to be created here. If they can agree on a price, then the actual settlement of the transaction can be deferred saving the seller the hassle and cost of car hire and the buyer the hassle of trying to find somewhere to park the car.

Of course, the parties still need to discuss cost. And the negotiation over price may be exactly the same as it would have been in a distributive negotiation. Perhaps they still arrive at a price of $22,500 but each party has saved time, money or stress.

In any negotiation, there will come a time where all the possible value has been created and the parties will need to claim their "fair share" of the value and move to distributive negotiation techniques. The challenge for the negotiator is to not move to these techniques too early.

E IS FOR ETHICS

Imagine you are selling your 10-year-old car. At the last service you are advised that the gearbox had some major issues and would probably need replacing within six months. You have a potential buyer who is willing to pay your asking price. They have not asked any questions about the condition of the car. Do you have an obligation to disclose the information about the gearbox?

What if the buyer asks "Are there any mechanical issues?" Does this change the situation?

What if the stakes are higher? Instead of selling a car with $10,000, you are selling a property worth $2 million and you know that Council is about to rezone the land?

These are all examples of ethical dilemmas that can exist in a negotiation. For some people, these scenarios may not provide an ethical dilemma at all. For others it may be quite a challenge to determine what is the right thing to do.

According to Lewicki[7], an ethical dilemma exists for a negotiator when *"possible actions or strategies put the potential economic benefits of doing a deal in conflict with one's social or moral obligations to other involved parties or one's broader community."* Given the very nature of most negotiations, this means it is almost impossible to avoid some degree of ethical dilemma in any negotiation.

In general, our choices in an ethical dilemma lie somewhere between "everyone should look out for themselves" and "I never lie". Rarely, is it black and white. Rather than "I never lie" it is more likely to be "I never lie unless...". We create our own caveats which are often subconscious and unrecognised but which justify small untruths or omissions.

Some ethical decisions may relate to illegal behaviour. Take for example, a company that hacks into the database of its takeover target to gain private information that will assist in its bid. Or the eco-warrior who trespasses on private property and chains himself to a tree to gather publicity and put pressure on the property developer to change their plans.

In general, most ethical choices in negotiation relate more to the decision to tell (or not tell) the truth. There are some negotiations where it is expected that a certain amount of bending of the truth will take place and it may not be considered unethical. Who, for example, has ever believed a car salesman who said "This is the lowest I can go."? What about the disgruntled supplier who makes an empty threat to sue for payment of a $200 bill?

Back in 1968, Carr[8] suggested that bluffing was a completely acceptable tactic in business negotiations. He likened it to "good poker playing". In fact, he went so far as to argue that if a business man (it was the 60's) failed to bluff he was probably "at a serious disadvantage in business dealings".

In the ensuing 50 years there have been both critics and supporters of Carr's position. Many critics argue that business people and corporations should be held to higher standards of ethical conduct.

At the end of the day, the question whether certain behaviours are ethical or not is generally going to be slightly grey. You may wish to apply the "billboard" test: When you head to work tomorrow morning, would you be happy to see your decision on a billboard at the side of the road? Would your action appear reasonable then?

F IS FOR FEAR OF FAILURE

Nobody sets out to fail. In fact, generally, people do everything in their power to avoid a failure. So once a negotiation has started, it can be easy to become wedded to achieving an agreement at all costs to ensure the negotiation is not a failure. Without careful analysis of the situation, this desire to avoid failure can lead to agreements which are not in your own best interest.

A story of failure

I was working with a client recently who wanted some guidance over a negotiation that had been going on for some time. My client was a director at an IT consulting company. The company had been working for a government department for several years, providing services in a specialist area. Twelve months previously, she had started negotiations with the department to take over all of the it's IT needs. After a year of ongoing negotiations, she was feeling stressed that she would have to report a failed negotiation to her bosses. She sought my advice on how to get the deal closed.

We started by looking at the interests of each party. My client needed to achieve certain KPIs and ultimately, wanted to ensure a deal which was profitable and long-term. The department wanted strong, consistent service with minimal disruption to the business.

Next we considered alternatives. We knew that if no agreement was reached, the department was likely to continue using the incumbent supplier. My client told me that the incumbent supplier had a long history working with the department and that as far as she knew, there were no quality issues. Based on the information she had, the competitor's pricing was aggressive and below what she could offer within her authorization levels.

As for the client's alternatives, she reported to me that the market was relatively buoyant. While there were not many contracts the size of the department's, she was confident that it would be relatively easy to secure three or four clients bringing in equal revenue. Given that there were no quality issues, it was going to be very difficult to convince the department's procurement team to accept a deal at a higher price.

After a thorough analysis of the situation, my client collated a report to management, justifying why the negotiation should be ended. Rather than reporting a 'failed negotiation" she reported a success. Time spent in the negotiation had built a strong relationship with the department, positioning the company well for future opportunities. Closing the negotiation now would allow the team to focus on winning other, more profitable deals.

Without having taken the time to analyse the situation in a structured way, the company could have continued to divert resources to a deal that wasn't going to succeed, missing valuable opportunities along the way.

Lessons learned

Two key lessons can be drawn from this example:

- Be careful how you define success - Success is not just about getting an agreement but is must be and agreement which is better than your best alternative.

- Applying a structured analysis to your negotiations will assist you in mitigating biases and blindspots in your negotiation and lead you to a better outcome.

G IS FOR GETTING TO YES

No discussion of negotiation would be fully complete without mention of the book Getting to Yes[9] by Roger Fisher and William Ury. First published in 1981, *Getting to Yes* sets out fundamental principles of interest-based negotiation. While some of the references within the book are now little dated, the foundation principles still remain current. I highly recommend it as a relatively easy read for anyone interested in in developing their negotiation skills.

For those of you who don't have the time to read the whole book, I've summarised below the key principles.

Separate the people from the problem

A key challenge in negotiations is the potential for high emotions. Often, this can result from poor communication or damaged relationships. When we separate the people from the problem, we use careful communication to ensure understanding. We also need to recognise that we can only ever make assumptions about a person's intention. All we can observe is the person's behaviour and the impact of that behaviour on us.

Focus on interests, not positions

This boils down to thinking not about what somebody wants but rather, why they want it. Take for example the classic story of two children fighting over an orange. If we asked the children what they wanted, both would say they want the orange. Based only on this information, the outcome might be to split the orange in half. Both children walk away feeling dissatisfied that they didn't get all of what they wanted. They may however feel satisfied that it was a "fair" outcome.

Imagine now, that we asked the children *why* they want the orange (that is, we dig for their interests). The first child tells us they are hungry. The second child tells us that they are making a Jaffa cake and they need some orange rind to flavour the chocolate batter that they've made.

Now that we focus on the interests, rather than the positions, a much better outcome becomes possible. We can grate the rind off the orange for the second child to use in the cake batter and give all of the orange flesh to the first child to eat.

Invent options for mutual gain

If we adopt a purely distributive negotiation process, it is very likely that the negotiation will result in a suboptimal outcome. Distributive negotiation often considers only one set of interests (often money) when parties may have significantly more interests play.

Take for example a new employee negotiating their salary. The employer has offered to pay $80,000 currently but the employee is requesting $85,000.

In a distributive negotiation, statistically they are likely end up with an agreed salary of around $82,500. However, let's assume that the employee has children in primary school. The employee pays around $60 a day for after-school care and feels slightly guilty about not being around much for the children. The employer could offer a day week working from home, saving the employee childcare costs of $2,880 over the year and providing additional time with the family. In theory, the employee could accept a salary of $82,120 and still be better off than if they got paid $85,000 with no working from home.

Insist on using objective criteria

Our brains are hardwired to look for reasons to do things. This is demonstrated in a famous Harvard study[10] where it was shown that the rate of agreement to a request to cutting in to the front of the photocopying line almost doubled when the requestor gave a reason for cutting in. This was despite the fact that the reason they gave was "because I need to make some copies" – a bogus reason.

Providing reasons for the requests we make in a negotiation assist in influencing our negotiation counterpart. The more objective these reasons, the more influential. So if you want to chop down a tree in your yard, saying to the council "I'd like to chop down a tree as I have an expert's report that it is structurally unsound" will be much more influential than "I'd like to chop down the tree as I'm worried about its safety".

Know your BATNA

BATNA is a commonly used negotiation acronym meaning *Best Alternative To a Negotiated Outcome*. In summary, we need to understand what we will do if we were unable to reach a negotiated outcome to determine what an acceptable negotiated outcome must look like. For more information about this, refer to *A is for Alternatives*.

H IS FOR HARD-BARGAINING

When I first started to learn about negotiation, I was basically told that hard-bargaining was unethical. That everyone should use interest-based bargaining. However, as I mentioned in *D is for Distributive Bargaining*, even in an interest-based negotiation, there will be a place for negotiating to claim your fair share of the value.

So, the question here is more about the tactics that negotiators may use to manipulate an outcome and whether or not you would choose to use them. Rather than hard-bargaining, I call these hardball tactics. Some of the most frequently cited hardball tactics you may come across are set out below.

- **Good cop / Bad cop** - Alternating between negotiators who use tough and more lenient negotiation approaches.

- **Lowball/Highball** - Using extreme offers to change the anchor of potential negotiation settlements.

- **Bogey** - Pretending a low priority item is important in order to trade it for a concession on another item.

- **Nibble** - Asking for a proportionally small concession on a new item to close the deal.

- **Chicken** - Using a large bluff plus a threat to force the other party to concede.

- **Intimidation** - Using emotional ploys such as anger and fear to force concessions.

- **Aggressive behaviour** - Relentless requests for more concessions and better deals with an aggressive tone.

- **Snow job** - Overwhelming the other party with so much information they can't make sense of it.

I'm certainly not advocating that you use any of these. In fact, I think the risk of them backfiring can be high. At a minimum, I'd be worried about my reputation as a negotiator by relying on these – although that is not something that seems to bother Donald Trump!

It is important to know how to defend yourself against these hardball tactics though. There are two pieces of overarching advice that may assist.

- **Be prepared** by knowing what the tactics are and stay alert during the negotiation to identify any possible tactics being used. I like to follow the advice we are all given for preventing terrorism – "Be alert, not alarmed".

- If you suspect the other party is using a tactic, **ask a question**. By seeking to get further explanations of certain offers or behaviour from your counterpart, you may place them in a position where they can no longer rely on the tactic

I IS FOR INTERESTS

Understanding interests is the key principle of the collaborative negotiation method set out in *Getting to Yes*. I've been biding my time through A to H of the alphabet, waiting to get to this central idea.

Interests are the needs, hopes, fears and concerns of the parties. What are the parties looking to achieve (or avoid) as an outcome of the negotiation? When we think of interests, we are thinking about the party's **motivation**.

It's important to distinguish between an interest and a **position**.

A position is **what** someone wants. An interest is **why** they want it. This difference is perhaps best illustrated by an example.

Imagine you are heading in to a negotiation with an existing customer. To make things simple, let's assume that the deal is done other than agreeing on what the payment terms will be. You go into the negotiation with a requirement that payment terms must be 14 days. This is a position, not an interest. The interests behind the position may be things like:

- I need to offer consistent terms to all customers

- I want to minimise my interest costs

- I want to demonstrate to my boss that I can achieve favourable outcomes for the company

- I've sold the company and want to minimise receivables at settlement date to avoid adjustments.

It is important to know the interests behind a position because it adds flexibility to the possible outcomes. As long as you know the interests you can meet, you can be flexible on how to meet them. For example, I may agree to 30 rather than 14 day terms but require a confidentiality clause or offer longer terms only for orders over a minimum amount. Or, I may offer a discount for payment within the 14 days so I can meet my settlement obligations.

When preparing for a negotiation it is important to consider your own interests. If you have an outcome in mind, why is this outcome important, what does it achieve for you?

You will also need to consider the other side's interests. What might they be seeking to achieve? If you can't offer them a deal that gets at least some of their key interests, you are unlikely to get a deal across the line. And the more of their interests you meet, the more likely you are to have a sustainable, productive deal.

The interests you consider should include both tangible and intangible interests. A tangible interest could be something like a profit margin or a deadline. Intangible interests may include things like protecting reputation or wanting simplicity in implementation.

It is also worthwhile considering different time frames. Some interests may be short term while others may impact over a longer timeframe.

By thinking about interests as broadly as possible, you open up the greatest scope for creating solutions that expand the amount of value to be claimed by both sides

Whether it's your own interests or the other parties, think beyond the obvious interests to some of the more intangible interests or perhaps longer term interests.

J IS FOR JUSTIFICATION

Recently, I was selling a sewing machine on eBay. It was pretty old and not in great condition so the listing price was a low $15. Given how the low the price was, I was pretty offended when I had a message from a buyer offering to buy it for $10. I mean seriously! What happened next though was a good bit of negotiation from my potential purchaser.

After I politely rejected the offer (saying that I was happy to wait two days for the end of the auction before considering their offer) the buyer came back with increased offer of $12 and an explanation for their offer – "I fix up vintage machines to teach kids sewing, this sounds like a cam problem, and parts unavailable so straight stitch ok. Have to travel 160kms for this one - hence my cheeky offer..".

What the buyer has done here is provide a justification or reason for the offer they have made. Not only did this change my attitude to them – I was no longer offended by their offer – but, knowing why they wanted to pay a low amount changed my behaviour too. I responded by saying that I would leave the auction open but if it didn't sell I was prepared to give them the machine for free. I could have chosen to get proof that what they said was true although frankly, for a $15 machine I was prepared to take the risk that they were lying.

If I was to give my buyer one piece of advice, it would be to give the explanation up front with the original offer. We know the human brain is primed to seek reasons for doing things (see the famous photocopier study by Ellen Langer[11]) so by just giving a reason for your offer, you increase the chance that it will be accepted.

Not only that, but by providing a logical reason for an offer that is below what the other party considers to be reasonable, you are able to mitigate any damage to the relationship.

Of course, when you are receiving an offer rather than making an offer, asking "what is the basis for that offer?" is a good way to move someone away from an unreasonable offer.

K IS FOR KAHNEMAN

Firstly, I have to confess that thinking of a "K" for negotiation was harder than it might seem. Every index of every textbook on my overloaded bookshelf seemed to jump from J to L as if K didn't even exist. However, a few of them made reference to Daniel Kahneman, best known for his book *Thinking Fast and Slow*[12]. Kahneman is generally regarded as the world's most influential living psychologist.

Most of Kahneman's work focuses on the difference between System 1 and System 2[13] thinking. In System 1 thinking, there is instinctive response and decisions are made very quickly. System 2 is a more structured thinking process and takes time to rationally investigate the whole scenario. In his work, Kahneman identifies many of the cognitive biases that have been mentioned in previous posts, such as anchoring, availability, loss aversion, framing and the sunk cost fallacy.

Also of relevance in the negotiation context is Kahneman's thinking around the difference between experience and memory which Kahneman himself discusses in his TED talk with almost 7 million views at the time of writing[14]..

When we negotiate with someone, that person has two versions of our negotiation – the lived experience and the memory of that experience.

This is of particular relevance to how we manage our reputation as a negotiator and how willing others may be to negotiate with us in the future.

Researchers have shown that in relation to any experience, the way the experience ends has a significant impact on our memory of that experience. For example, Kahneman talks about two colonoscopy patients. The first patient has a shorter procedure but the final part of the procedure is where the patient experiences the most pain. The second patient has a much longer procedure and experiences significantly more pain than the first patient, however there pain reaches its peak in the middle of the procedure. In the patients' memories, the first patient reports a worse experience than the second, even though they had less overall pain.

While everyone experiences a negotiation, our memory may distort how we see that negotiation in the future. A tough negotiation that ends with some friendly, positive comments may get you better long-term results than a very friendly negotiation that turns hostile when agreement cannot be reached.

Taking the time to ensure a negotiation finishes positively, even when it has been difficult, will be a worthwhile investment.

L IS FOR LISTENING

To be an expert negotiator, one must be a great listener. Too often, we see people trying to negotiate by telling the other side why what they want makes sense. We know that people value autonomy and the mere fact we tell someone what to do can reduce our chances of them actually doing it.

Why should we listen?

If we can effectively listen to our negotiation counterpart we can achieve 3 key benefits.

Understanding

Negotiation is the exercise of trying to change someone's mind. How can you change someone's mind if you don't know where it's at?

Connection

Relationship is a critical part of successful negotiation. Listening can assist us in building rapport and, importantly, builds trust.

Reciprocity

We increase the chance that they will listen to us. Just as we may be tempted to focus the negotiation airtime on convincing the other party that we are right, our counterpart may be seeking to do the same. By giving them that airtime and showing we have listened, we increase the chances that they will be prepared to listen to our perspective.

How do we listen better?

So if we can agree that listening is important, the question becomes how do we get better at it. While hearing is a sense and happens automatically, listening is a skill. It is the ability to take what we hear and make sense of it. As with all skills, listening needs to be practiced to be done well.

Here's a few key tips to improve your listening skills.

Listen to understand

Think about recent negotiations you've had. As your counterpart was speaking were you busy already trying to formulate your reply or focusing on all the objections you had to what they were saying? While these are important activities, see if you can defer them until after the person has finished speaking. Focus on understanding what is being said before seeking to respond.

Your focus during listening should be on the speaker rather than your own thoughts and emotions.

Listen for what's not being said

In a negotiation, it is important not just to hear the words that are being spoken but to pay attention to what has not been said. It might be that the other side is deliberately leaving information out and using vague wording – the ultimate trick of politicians.

We also need to interpret the needs and emotions that underlie what is being said. Understanding emotions is critical in many negotiations. If we fail to address these intangible interests, even the most rational of solutions will be ignored.

Listen to yourself

One of the challenges of effective listening is that our minds are so busy thinking all the time. In order to listen, we need to quiet that internal chatter. Before we enter a negotiation, making time to sit in silence for a minute or two and recognise what's going on in our own minds can help us to clear the space to listen effectively in the negotiation.

There is no doubt that effective listening can be challenging but it's certainly a skill worth developing.

M IS FOR MESO

Ok, first things first here - we are not talking about soup!

In negotiation, we know that understanding the interests of the other party is critical to enable us to maximise value. We also know that while a party may have many interests, some of these will be more important to them than others. MESOs are a tool for assisting us to understand the relative importance of various interests to our negotiation counterpart.

MESO stands for **Multiple Equivalent Simultaneous Offers**. The idea behind the concept is that by putting forward multiple options to the other side, their response will give you more information about how the other side is prioritising its interests.

By providing a set of different options to the other party, we can use their responses to the options to identify their priorities. The key to using MESOs is that the different options we put forward should all be of equivalent value to us.

How to prepare MESOs

Imagine you are selling computer packages to corporate customers and you want to craft a MESO to put on the table.

Step 1: Identify your priorities.

So to start, we need to identify our own priorities. In this case, it may be that the unit price, timing of the sale, after sales service and future sales are all relevant.

Step 2: Create a scoring system

By allocating weighting to each of the priorities, you are able to create a scoring system to allow you to measure the value of different combinations of options.

Step 3: Create equivalent offers

Based on your scoring system, come up at least two offers which are of equivalent value to you but would meet the other party's interests differently. You may come up with a few different pairs of offers to test a number of potential interests.

Step 4: Put each offer forward separately

Rather than putting all the different options forward at once, you want to put two offers forward at a time. There should only be one key difference between each offer if possible so the response to the offer will give you a clear indication of the other party's interest.

A bit like an optometrist checking your eyes, each choice between pairs of offers will bring you clarity around what is important to the other party.

An example

Say you were selling computer packages and a customer has indicated they want 1,000 units. The various factors that are important to you may include: unit price, timing, locations, future sales and follow up service. Rather than offering a single offer to a potential customer, you could provide several offers which all give you the same amount of value. For example, the first options could be:

- 100 units at $1,000 each to be provided now on a sale only basis

- 100 units at $950 with a $100 per unit 12 month service contract.

If the customer expresses interest in the second option, even if they are not happy with the price, you get information that service is an interest for them and you can work this in to further options. You may then look at the possibility of future business by providing further options, say:

- 100 units at $950 with a $100 per unit 12 month service contract

- 100 units at $900 with a $100 per unit 12 month service contract and a commitment to replace all units after 2 years

From the customer's response to these options, you will be able to get a sense of whether the client values a long term relationship.

When using MESOs it is important to leave some room for negotiation rather than putting your best offer on the table. You are trying to get information rather than a firm commitment at this stage. MESOs can also add complexity to a negotiation so avoid putting more than three options on the table at any time.

N IS FOR NO

H ave you ever found yourself in a conversation where you've said yes when you really wanted to say no? I know I have. In fact, I once found myself on a over 50's bus trip around the Northern Territory with my grandfather because I didn't know how to say "no". Now there's an embarrassing story for another day![15]

So why is it so hard to say no? Well, the short answer is fear or anger get in our way. Either way, we end up with a result that is not great for us. Let's have a look at that in more detail.

What happens when we don't say "no"?

Generally, if we don't say no we will go to one of three alternatives.

- We **Avoid** – here's where we dodge the conversation so we don't have to say yes or no. While we avoid confrontation we also don't get any resolution, most likely causing stress and frustration for both parties – and damaging the relationship.

- We **Attack** – in this case, we do provide a "no" but we do using raised voices or angry words. Words may be said in the heat of the moment which we later regret – and can't take back! Of course, the result is a damaged relationship.

- We **Accommodate** – in this case, fear stops us from saying no so we just agree to what is being asked of us to avoid damaging the relationship. (That's what happened with my grandfather – who also used a bit of emotional blackmail to make the stakes higher*). Of course, this sets a precedent for future interactions in which we are likely to continue a pattern of accommodating which leads to a growing sense of frustration for us – and we end up damaging the relationship.

What we often see is an escalation from one approach to another. Most common may be starting with avoiding the negotiation altogether. When the other person pushes the issue you may attack, telling them how unreasonable they are for pressuring you. If they persist in pushing things, you may revert to accommodate – it's just easier to cave in.

So how do I say no?

Firstly, you need to know that this won't always be easy. However, to increase your change of success and decrease your stress, here's a few tips.

Slow things down

When you get a request that makes you feel uncomfortable saying no to, take a short break. Taking time out to find out why you are hesitant and what it is about this request that is creating some emotional response in you will help you avoid caving in too soon or jumping in to attack mode.

Start with yourself

Be clear on what is important to you. When you want to say no to something it is often because it conflicts with your needs, interests or values. Taking the time to clearly think about what these are can help you articulate why "no" is so important for you. It also gives you the confidence to "stick to your guns" (apologies for the adversarial analogy in a non-adversarial process).

Listen and demonstrate your understanding

While you may not *agree* with what the other party believes, it is important to fully *understand* what they believe. If the other party doesn't feel heard they will most likely keep pushing, believing that you are saying "no" as you haven't properly understood them.

You can demonstrate that you understand them without actually agreeing with them. This removes the resistance we often see when someone feels they are not being listened to. For example: "What I hear you saying is that the goods were expected to be delivered in a reasonable timeframe. You needed the goods in two days and you believe that the delivery in three days was unreasonable."

Think of the other person

Understanding the impact of your "no" on the other person is important. Are you saying "no, not at all" or "no, not this way". Conveying the message that you are open to finding other ways to meet the other person's interests as well as your own will be helpful. Ask them to treat your "no" as the beginning of a negotiation.

Remember, the other person will often be accountable to other stakeholders. Helping them to find ways to frame their acceptance of your "no" to these stakeholders will also help them to save face and make your "no" more palatable.

O IS FOR OPTIONS

I remember when I first started learning about negotiating, being introduced to the concept of Pareto efficiency with a fairly complicated graph and a bit of economic theory. In fact, over the years, I have introduced this same graph and theory to many of my workshop participants. For today, I'm going to save you the graph and theory but give you the headline concepts you need to think about.

We often focus on getting to an agreement in a negotiation. In doing so, both sides may put various offers on the table. Each of these is an "option" in negotiation speak – it is a possible outcome that the parties could agree to as a commitment in the negotiation. With options being put back and forth between the parties, it is usual that as soon as an option is put by one party that is acceptable to the other party, the music stops and we move towards implementing the agreement.

This is all good, after all a deal has been done and we should be happy. But there's a problem. In agreeing to the first acceptable option, the parties have got to "Yes" but have they got to the best "Yes" possible?

Take the following example. Jake and Fiona both operate manufacturing businesses in a rural city. After several conversations and some engineering inspections, Jake agree to buy a piece of machinery from Fiona for $100,000. The machinery will be delivered in two months. They are both comfortable with the price and the delivery timeframe. The sale is documented and the parties get on with their business pending the transfer date.

In the meantime, Jake has to send several of his staff off to be trained in how to use the machine. He loses valuable production time as the training is 4 hours away and he also incurs travel and accommodation costs. Also, he's really frustrated at the delivery delay because he's got orders waiting to be started. For Fiona, she's got customer commitments that require the use of the machinery for the two month period but only at a reduced capacity. She stopped taking orders when she decide to sell. So, now the machine is taking up space on the factory floor but is idle for a large part of the time. And, she's paying for a full-time operator who she can't make redundant until after the machine sale completes.

If the parties had shared their concerns about missed sales and underutilized staff, a much better option could have been reached. For example, Jake could have sent staff to Fiona's factory for on site training, commencing production on the stock that Jake wants to make. Fiona could have recouped some of her labour costs and Jake could have gotten stock much faster.

A good thing to do in negotiation is to take a pause once an outcome is reached. Agree that this is a minimum outcome but keep the conversation going to see how it might be improved.

P IS FOR PREPARATION

"The problem is not usually faulty preparation,
but a lack of preparation at all"

This quote from Deepak Malhotra in his book, Negotiation Genius is a pretty good reflection of what happens in many negotiations. Due to the time pressures on the participants, it is all too common for parties to start a negotiation by winging it, relying on past experience and expertise in a very unstructured way.

Where preparation does occur before the negotiation, it often focuses on the **what** of the negotiation – what information do I need to know, what are my budgets, what is the impact of success/failure. Parties think about the content of the negotiation without always considering the process – or **how** they will negotiate. This latter element is often the difference between a good negotiator and a great one.

Like with most things in life, a little preparation can go a long way in a negotiation. While there are many things to consider before getting into a negotiation, I've summarised the preparation into four basic areas.

Who

Before starting, think about whether you are the correct person to be doing this negotiation. Is there someone more skilled or who has a better relationship to the other party. For example, where you are emotionally attached to an outcome, having a more neutral party assisting in the negotiation may be beneficial.

Think also about who is the correct person to be negotiating with on the other side. Is the person the ultimate decision maker? Do you have a good relationship with them or is there an alternative person who may be easier to negotiate with.

One of my clients was a banker working in the farming sector. He had been struggling with his negotiations with some of the farmers. It was only when he realised that he needed to include the farmers' wives in the discussion that his results improved! Although on paper, they didn't own the farm, they were critical to major decisions being made.

What?

This is the part where you prepare your content. Do you have all your facts to hand? Are you across all the background? Do you have enough data to support your position?

One of the challenges here is we tend to only look for the data which supports what we want. To be truly effective, you should also intentionally look for data that supports the other party's position. Doing so may reduce your risk of getting surprised in the negotiation.

It is also important to think here about what happens if you don't reach agreement. Knowing the alternatives is critical to determining when to exit the negotiation rather than agreeing to something that doesn't best suit your needs.

Why?

At the heart of negotiation is understanding interests. Ensure you know not just the outcome you are hoping for but also why that is important to you. What are the underlying interests that you are trying to satisfy.

I once mediated a dispute about ownership of some video footage of pro-wrestling. Both parties were seeking ownership of the footage. In private sessions, I asked the parties why they needed the footage. They needed to stop and reflect on this for a while but the first party told me they only wanted it to make sure the other party didn't get it. The second party wanted it because he didn't want to redo his website which contained some short snippets of the footage.

We quickly came to an arrangement where the first party retained ownership but granted a licence to the second party for the footage on their website. If they had focused on their "why" earlier, both parties could have saved thousands of dollars in legal fees and a lot of stress.

How?

This is the process piece of the puzzle. Negotiators need to plan for the way in which they prepare to negotiate. This can include a range of strategies to think about:

- When is the best time to schedule the negotiation? Will you arrive early, on time or late?

- Where should the negotiation be held? Choosing the location of one of the parties or a neutral location may signal something to the other party.

- How should seating be arranged at the meeting?

- How will you structure the negotiation? Having a clear idea of an agenda for the discussions is a critical part of managing the negotiation.

- Will you be the first to put an offer on the table? Knowing the right time to make an offer and how to structure your offer effectively can have a big impact on the final result.

For many negotiators, planning is impacted by time constraints. However, if the negotiation outcomes are important to you, investing the time, and seeking support from third parties who can bring a different perspective, is well worth it.

Q IS FOR QUIET

On page 36 of this book I discussed how listening is a critical part of skilled negotiation. It goes without saying that to listen effectively, you need to be quiet. In this section, I want to look a little deeper in other benefits of taking a quieter approach to negotiation.

Quiet builds relationships

Whether you are naturally quieter or have to work hard to be so, focusing on taking a quieter role in the conversation can assist you in building deeper connections with your counterpart.

Many people enter a negotiation with a degree of fear or concern. This can set up a fight or flight response which leads to sub-optimal negotiation behaviours. If you can make them feel safe, listened to and valued, you will reduce the chances that they will have this response. A more open conversation is likely to result.

Quiet can slow things down

On the face of it, slowing things down may seem counterproductive. After all, we all live in a busy, busy world and time seems to be in short supply. However, what we often see in business is that decisions made in a rush tend to not be fully implemented or problems turn up in the implementation process. We then need to go back to the drawing board spending more time to get things right.

Slowing down from the start may mean decisions take longer, but should result in better decisions.

Quiet learns more

One of the sayings I use in most of my workshops is "*When you speak you repeat what you already know. When you listen, you may learn something new*". This is one of the big advantages of being quiet during a negotiation.

Interestingly, we are all impacted by a psychological bias that causes us to focus on finding information which confirms our beliefs. We therefore can come into a negotiation not only believing that we are "right" but also that we have all the relevant information.

It can seem pointless to listen to the other side because we know they are wrong and they won't convince us otherwise. If we consciously decide to quietly listen for a while, we may just discover that there is indeed other information and perhaps we weren't as "right" as we thought.

If we are really lucky, we may even learn something that allows us to create an even better deal than what we had planned.

What is your experience of switching to quiet in a negotiation? Is it something that comes naturally or something you need to work at?

R IS FOR REFLECTION

In a busy world where everyone is bombarded by emails, calls, meetings and various other demands on their time, finding the time for reflection can be a challenge. However, reflection is the key to improving your negotiation skills. It is only by taking time after each negotiation to look at how it went that you can build the skills that help you get better.

Taking into account the challenges of finding time, I offer two separate models for reflecting on your negotiations which will assist in your development. The choice you make will depend on how much time you have.

A quick reflection

After every negotiation, I recommend asking these two basic questions:

- **What worked well and what didn't work well?** What were the things you (or the other side) did that helped to achieve an outcome, increase overall value or claim value? On the flip side, what things happened that caused problems in the negotiation or gave away value unnecessarily?

- **Why did those things work or not work?** This is critical. Some techniques will work in some situation but not in others. Recognising what it is about the situation that makes a technique work or fail allows you to make choices in future negotiations about the appropriateness of a particular technique. Using the old tool box analogy, I may be an expert in using screwdrivers but using a screwdriver to hammer in a nail probably won't work!

A longer reflection

If you have more time available, then a more structured reflection may be helpful. I follow a reflection model based around the Harvard 7 Elements model.

Commitment

- Did you have the right decision makers involved in the process?

- Did you seek agreement on how you would negotiate as well as on the outcomes?

- Is there any risk that the agreements you arrived at could be misconstrued or that the parties will be unable to deliver?

Relationship

- Was the relationship improved or damaged by the negotiation? Why?

- Did you clarify any assumptions you had about their intentions?

Communication

- How well did you do at listening without interrupting or thinking of responses before the other person finished speaking?

- Did you check in to ensure your understanding of key points was correct and that they understood your key points?

Interests

- Were you able to communicate clearly your underlying interests in a way which helped them to meet your needs (without giving away your weaknesses)?

- Were you able to glean from them their underlying interests.

Options

- Did you explore a range of options before committing to try to maximise value?

- Once you reached an agreement, did you keep working to see if that base agreement could be improved upon?

Standards

- Did you come prepared with data and evidence to support your negotiations?

- Did you ask them for justifications for offers they were proposing?

Alternatives

- Did you consider your best-case alternative if an agreement was not able to be reached?

- Did you agree to something that was at least as good as that alternative?

- Did you consider what their best-case alternative was in the event of no agreement being reached?

An important consideration in your reflection is being totally honest with yourself. This is not the time to justify every move you made in the negotiation but to honestly reflect and critique. I always encourage sharing these reflections as well. If team members share their learning, then everyone in the team can benefit from the learning and the group will all build their skills.

S IS FOR STYLE

—••●◉●••—

Now, I'm not suggesting here that you need to be "stylish" to be a good negotiator but you do need to understand the different negotiation styles. Knowing your default style and recognising others' styles will assist you in being flexible in negotiations to get the best outcome in different situations.

Many people are now familiar with the Thomas Kilmann Conflict Styles[16] model. This focuses on how individuals react in times of conflict. Do they compete, compromise, avoid, accommodate or collaborate?

Negotiation Styles Model

Because in general, people consider conflict as a different concept to negotiation, I prefer to use the work of Laurie R. Weingart who proposes a model of four negotiation styles. This more closely aligns with the non-dispute based negotiations.

Weingart's model proposes four negotiation styles:

- **Individualists** focus on maximising their own outcomes. They show little concern for others' outcomes. Instead of creating value, individualists tend to claim it, argue their positions forcefully, and, at times, make threats.

- **Cooperators** focus on maximising their own and their counterparts' results. Cooperators are more open to strategies that create value—such as exchanging information and making multi-issue offers—than individualists are.

- **Competitives** are motivated to maximise the difference between their own and others' outcomes. For them, winning is a relative concept. In order to out-do the competition, competitives tend to engage in behavior that's self-serving and that blocks collaborative solutions.

- **Altruists** strive to maximize their counterparts' outcomes rather than their own. Though few of us are pure altruists, virtually everyone behaves altruistically under certain conditions, as when dealing with loved ones or those less fortunate than we are.

While we don't have any Australian research of the prevalence of these different styles, US research indicates that the split is over 50% of negotiators are individualists, 25-35% cooperators, 5-10% competitives with a handful of altruists thrown in the mix.

While no one style is "better" than another most research suggests that negotiators with a primarily cooperative style are more successful than hard bargainers at reaching novel solutions that improve everyone's outcomes. Negotiators who lean toward cooperation also tend to be more satisfied with the process and their results, according to Weingart. This is the style of negotiation that I focus on teaching.

That being said, claiming value and lobbying tenaciously for your position can be equally important negotiation strategies. As with many things in life, balance is the key - focus on building a cooperative relationship and creating value, then work to claim as much as you can of that value for yourself.

So what do you think your preferred negotiation style is?

T IS FOR THREATS

It is unlikely that you will get through too many negotiations without facing a counterpart who tries to use threats to improve their own outcome.

From a clear ultimatum – "Drop your prices by 15% or we're taking our business elsewhere" – to a more subtle threat - "It would be a shame if details of this issue were to find their way to the press" - threats are used by negotiators to demonstrate their power and to claim value for themselves.

Expert negotiators need to both defuse a threat made by their counterpart as well as knowing when and how to make threats themselves.

How to defuse a threat

When a counterpart issues a threat to you in the negotiation, the first thing to remember is that, generally, threats represent the party's best alternative if an agreement is not reached.

So, if you're trying to collect payment on a debt, and believe you've got a rock solid case in court, you may threaten to sue me if you don't agree to payment of a certain amount. For you, if you can't get at least $x now, you'd be better off by going to court.

Every party in every negotiation has a best alternative so I can simply acknowledge that fact and try to get the negotiation back on track. "Of course you could sue us, and we feel we could sue you for the poor quality of the goods you but rather than focusing on that, we'd like to discuss how we can come up with a result today that saves both of us the time and stress of litigating this."

If the threat keeps coming up, you may try another tactic to defuse the threat by testing it against how well it meets your counterpart's interests or if it is realistic. For example, "I know you could sue us but we're offering to settle?" or "I understand you could sue us and our advice is that the recent changes to the legislation have changed the position around this and that we have no case to answer".

How to make a threat

When I first started teaching negotiation, it was suggested to me that threats had no place in an interest-based negotiation and should be avoided at all costs. However, there are definitely times when introducing a threat into the situation can deliver you a better result and maybe move the other party away from a stubborn position and firmly back to the deal table.

Before launching a threat, it is useful to consider three key questions:

What's my purpose?

Why am I considering this threat? If the answer is that you are angry and the threat is an emotional reaction to this action, the best plan is generally to avoid the threat. Anger is an emotion which can lead to poor judgement and risky behaviour. If anger is taking over, a better strategy is to take a break in the negotiation and give yourself time to calm down.

What could they threaten?

Think about what alternatives the other party could have that they have not raised. If their possible threats are bigger than yours, it may be best to keep yours to yourself.

Does the threat promote your interests?

Making a threat to harm or offend the other party is quite possibly going to do more damage to your position than leaving it unsaid. If your threat angers the other party and makes them less collaborative in the negotiation, your chances of getting to an acceptable outcome may have been reduced rather than enhanced.

Is there a way you can frame the threat as something that helps their interest rather than hurting them? For example, "If your refusal to negotiate forces us to bankruptcy, it's unlikely you'll see much of the money you are owed but if we can work together to find a way to continue business and protect your future debts then we can work with you to promote your product in the market.".

U IS FOR ULTIMATUMS

W̲e have all been in negotiations where an ultimatum has been put on the table – "This is my final offer, take it or leave it!"

Ultimatums are generally issued to bring the negotiation to a close or to signal power, but are they something we should use? And if our counterpart puts an ultimatum on the table, how should we respond?

What's the problem with an ultimatum?

It is not uncommon for some of my clients in mediations to start with an ultimatum. "I'm not walking out of here with a cent less than $x" or "If they think I'm going to pay them a cent then we're all wasting out time." Parties often come in to the negotiation thinking that this tough stance will scare the other party and help to get a better outcome for themselves.

The main difficulty this is that it sets up another key interest in the negotiation – Ego. Once a negotiator issues an ultimatum, they now have an interest in saving face and not being seen to back down.

In reality, most ultimatums are not issued as serious threats. They are a tactic rather than an indication that the party will walk away from the negotiation if their demand is not met. However, once the ultimatum is issued, how can the party walk away from it without looking like they have caved in? Now they are locked into a position which is not helpful to them but they can't move without looking weak.

So, how do I respond to an ultimatum?

Like with many unhelpful things in life, we can choose to ignore an ultimatum. If the ultimatum is real, you can rest assured, it will be repeated over and over again and you will have another chance to respond. If it is not real, by responding to it, you give it more strength than it deserves.

Ignore it

Assume that you repeat the ultimatum or ask the other party to clarify it. They now have a clear signal that you have heard the ultimatum and in increased interest in not backing down. By moving the conversation on without acknowledging the ultimatum, we take some of its power away.

Reframe it

If ignoring the ultimatum is not possible - perhaps it's been repeated a couple of times - you may need to reframe it in a way which creates space for the other person to back down without losing face.

For example, you might respond with "I understand that based on where things are at the moment, it would be difficult for you to agree to less than that today."

This statement does two things. Firstly, it reframes an absolute no to a mere difficulty – it would be hard but not impossible. Secondly, it suggests that the no is only valid at a point in time and may change.

Should I issue an ultimatum?

There is always a choice to issue an ultimatum and there may be times when doing so may be helpful to you. Perhaps some show of power is needed to get the negotiation moving.

While I rarely advise that you never do something, I will recommend that you ask the following questions before issuing an ultimatum:

- Am I prepared for the fact that they may take the ultimatum seriously and close down the negotiation? If they do this, am I prepared for the consequences. If this is a dispute situation, perhaps I'll find myself out of negotiations and into a costly legal dispute.

- How will I back down from the ultimatum without losing face? If I back down on this, will they believe me on other areas of the negotiation or just assume I am playing hardball.

- What will be the impact on our negotiation relationship?

V IS FOR VALUE

Many people see the goal as a negotiation being the idea of reaching agreement. While agreement is obviously the end goal of a negotiation, the idea of building value through negotiation is often overlooked. Parties will reach agreement, do the deal and move on.

According to the late Professor Howard Raiffa, a former professor at Harvard Business School, negotiation should be focused not on getting an outcome but "toward the question of how to create **joint value**."

Take for example the following situation. Spencer is selling his car and Bridget wants to buy it. Spencer wants to get $20,000 for the car but Bridget offers $17,000. If the goal is simply to get to agreement, the parties are likely to haggle on price until they reach a number that is acceptable to both. Research tells us that is likely to be around the mid-point between the first offer made in the negotiation and the first counter-offer. Let's say around $18,500 in this case.

However, imaging that in a search for value, the parties spend time uncovering each others' interests. Spencer learns that Bridget isn't really wanting a car just yet because she lives in a flat with no parking space. She started looking as she's moving in about 6 weeks and will need a car then. But she likes this model and colour so thought she'd come and have a look. If necessary, she can rent a car space if she really likes the car.

Bridget learns that Spencer is selling his car because he's moving overseas in two months. He started the sales process early so he wouldn't be forced into a discount sale to get in done before he leaves but will have to hire a car before he leaves if he sells now.

Also inspiring Spencer to start the sale process now rather than closer to his departure date is the fact that the registration is due in one month. He would rather avoid having to pay the registration out of his cash reserves.

Knowing these factors, the parties are able to come up with a better deal than an immediate sale at $18,500. They agree that Bridget will buy the car but in only in six week's time when she has to move. She will pay a deposit on the car and agrees that Spencer can use that deposit to cover the cost of registration. She is willing to cover the costs of registration from the date of transfer and Spencer will cover the costs until then. Not only that, but Bridget will also buy some of Spencer's appliances and furniture that he is selling as she needs to furnish her new place and his stuff looks great.

Both parties are much happier – and better off - than if they had simply traded the car for money.

As a negotiator, your job should always be to look for ways to find value in the deal. Being prepared to share what is important to you, and being curious about what is important to the other party is the best way to facilitate this process.

W IS FOR WINNER'S CURSE

Imagine you are in the midst of purchasing a new house. There's no auction but the agent asks for offers. You submit your offer but the agent comes back and tells you there's a higher offer. You really want the house so you increase the offer. There's another counter offer and you put in yet another offer. It's a bit above what you wanted to pay but you really want the house. The agents very quickly come back and accept your offer. Chances are, you will walk away from the negotiation feeling a little dissatisfied even if you're happy to buy the house.

This is the phenomenon know as the Winner's Curse. Often, when multiple people or businesses are vying for the same thing, the winner of the auction is revealed to have been overly optimistic about the value of the item and is a victim of the "winner's curse," Typically this is described as paying more than the asset is actually worth.

While I have used the example of buying a house, the winner's curse can often be seen in competitive tender situations as well. Given the desire to win the tender, tenderers can reduce the price to a point where they win the work but make so little margin that it isn't really worth the effort.

In these competitive situations, there a few things you can consider in advance to minimise your risk of suffering from the curse.

Know your interests

Not all assets are valued purely for their economic value. Take for example, a house which is valued at $1 million by an independent valuer. A buyer purchasing solely for an investment will be basing value on rental yields and capital growth. The $1 million may make sense. But, for a buyer who has an emotional connection to the house – perhaps it was built by an ancestor and they want it back in the family – a higher price may still represent good value. Or, for someone who desperately wants to have a house on top of a hill with a view, this view may justify a price above what others consider rational.

By being clear about your interests in advance of the bidding process, you can be clear why the value to you may be justifiably higher than others are willing to pay.

Understand your knowledge

You may be in a position where you are in a privileged position to understand more about the real value of the asset. Others may be basing their value on different knowledge. Take for example an auction of estate jewellery. Many may be bidding based only on the current value of gold and the precious stones and the resale value. If you have specialist knowledge and understand that this piece has a historical significance based on its history, then it is natural you will pay more than others are willing to pay.

Prepare for the win

By its nature, an auction winner has paid more than anyone else thinks the item is worth (or can afford). Reminding yourself of that in advance and sticking to the limits you have set yourself can assist in avoiding the Winner's Curse.

Y IS FOR YES

The obvious choice here for Y was "Yes" but I think this overlooks a really important piece of the negotiation equation – You. Sometimes, the only thing standing in the way of a good negotiation is the stories that are going on in your own head.

In his book, *Getting to Yes with Yourself*[17], William Ury talks about the need to focus on the inner game of negotiation. He tells us that you can't get to yes with your counterparts if you haven't been able to get to yes with yourself.

Ury shares one of my favourite quotes from Theodore Roosevelt who is reported to have said "If you could kick the person in the pants responsible for most of your trouble, you wouldn't sit for a month".

So what do we need to do to put ourselves out of our own way in a negotiation? There's a few tips that can help you.

Dig down to find your "why"

Just as you would empathetically listen to a friend who has a need or a problem, take the time to listen to yourself empathetically. Don't start by negatively judging yourself.

Move away from blame

It is all too easy to blame others for the difficult situation we find ourselves in. Taking more responsibility and focusing on what we can do to take care of our situation, regardless of the actions others do or do not take, can be a challenge but will position you well in your negotiations.

Change the frame

Most negotiations involve an element of scarcity. Something we want isn't available easily. This scarcity can invoke fear and start neurological changes which make rational thought difficult. Reframing the way we see things can assist. Rather than fearing scarcity, seeing life as "being on your side" can help you manage your state.

Learn to focus on now

When in a negotiation, particularly a dispute, it is easy to focus on what has gone on in the past and the conflict that has arisen. Or perhaps you will move to a place where your focus is on the uncertain future. Both can raise cortisol and adrenaline which will not aid your negotiations. Learning to stay focused on the present moment will move you in the right direction.

Don't make it personal

Others may make personal attacks in a negotiation and raise the tension. It can be easy to fall into the trap of retaliation – psychological mirroring plays a big part here. Being mindful enough to recognise what is going on and avoid unconsciously reflecting their behaviour will protect you.

Ury advises we "surprise others with respect and inclusion *even if* they are difficult".

Be the change

You may feel concerned where there are limited resources that you need to protect what you have. This can see the negotiation falling in to the win-lose game. Strategically starting the game by giving something away can see the rules change.

Z IS FOR ZZZZZ

Some of you may be wondering what sleep has to do with negotiation. When we negotiate, we need to be mentally prepared and in a state which allows us to stay focused and think on our feet. These are all things that will be adversely impacted by insufficient sleep.

When you're sleepy, most of your cognitive abilities reduce. For example:

- Speed of processing information slows down.

- Ability to multitask weakens.

- Ability to organize information and concepts into categories breaks down.

- Ability to recognise patterns withers.

- Ability to change your mind is inhibited.

- Ability to remember instructions long enough to accomplish a task dissolves.

Cognition defines how you understand a particular situation and how you act as a result. It affects what you see, what you hear, how you remember events, and how you react to those events.

A loss of cognitive abilities can affect critical elements of negotiation abilities:

- Perception

- Language skills

- Motor skills

- Social skills

Sleep Restores Creativity

Interest based negotiation relies on creatively brainstorming options to increase the amount of value on the table. When well rested, you are most likely more creative than when you're tired. When well rested, a negotiator can contemplate new solutions to seal a deal and be able to consider the effects of putting into practice those suggestions.

Sleep-Deprived People are More Likely to Cheat

According to a Harvard Business Review report, sleep deprived people are more likely to cheat. Lack of sleep may cause an otherwise moral person to engage in unethical practices. Unethical behavior can damage relations and cause legal problems.

Lack of sleep affects how we exercise willpower and self-control. We are then more at risk of resorting to unethical shortcuts to achieve temporary results. For example, it may be tempting to oversell your proposition or lie about the fine print of a contract.

Sleepiness Can Result in Memory Loss

The quantity and quality of sleep can have a profound effect on memory retention. When you're sleep deprived, you may struggle through the three stages of memory.

- Acquisition: You may find it challenging to grasp new information.

- Consolidation: Your brain may struggle to stabilize memories.

- Recall: You could find it challenging to access stored information.

While acquisition and recall only happen during wakefulness, consolidation occurs when you sleep. While asleep, the brain strengthens neural connections which stabilize your memories.

Lack of sleep can interrupt the consolidation phase. Interruption of neural connections hampers the acquisition and recall processes. Therefore, a negotiator lacking sleep will likely find it challenging to keep up with discussions. When deprived of sleep, it's common to miss conversation details that are critical to the deal.

Sleep Deprivation Can Cause Anger

Sleep affects your mood. Poor sleep patterns, not enough sleep, or low quality of sleep can all result in stress and feeling irritable. Sleep deprivation may cause you to be abrupt and unsociable. This leads to mistrust and loss of goodwill.

An irritable negotiator may react harshly to the slightest provocation. Your anger may result in turning down a great deal for personal reasons unrelated to the agreement.

Fatigue Prompts Anxiety

Negotiation trainers often warn trainees about being prone to bouts of anxiety if they are sleep deprived in a high-tension negotiation environment. It's a vicious cycle. Anxiety heightens insomnia, often leading to more sleepiness and more anxiety. Lack of sleep and anxiety feed off each other, which worsens the situation.

A tired negotiator fighting anxiety can end up accepting an unfavorable offer. For instance, you may accept an offer at a seemingly acceptable purchase price without factoring in shipping and handling expenses.

ABOUT THE AUTHOR

Nicole Davidson is a specialist in negotiation and alternative dispute resolution. She coaches individuals and groups to improve their outcomes and runs group training to build skills.

As a qualified lawyer and a former insolvency practitioner and investment banker, Nicole brings a wealth of real world experience to her negotiation practice.

She left insolvency practice ten years ago to focus on the skills based elements of business rather than the technical elements. She has held positions as Learning and Development Manager in a range of professional service firms as well as working with specialist leadership training consultancies.

In her current work, Nicole focuses on bringing an understanding of the dynamics of negotiations and business relationships to assist clients in negotiating better outcomes and in resolving disputes in a way which preserves relationships. She also believes that there are faster, cheaper and more effective ways of resolving disputes than by going to court. Because of this, she is an accredited mediator, helping parties to resolve disputes, before or during the litigation process. She also coaches clients to reduce the risk of conflicts arising.

Throughout her career, Nicole has worked across a broad range of industries. She quickly and easily learns and adapts to new environments. She also regularly practices negotiation skills with her lawyer husband and her three children.

- www.nicoledavidsonnegotiation.com.au

- https://www.facebook.com/nicoledavidsonnegotiation

- https://www.nicoledavidsonnegotiation.com.au/blog-1

ENDNOTES

1   https://www.linkedin.com/pulse/power-negotiation-taking-control-how-cookie-crumbles-nicole-davidson/?published=t

2   Pinkley, Robin. (1995). *Impact of Knowledge Regarding Alternatives to Settlement in Dyadic Negotiations: Whose Knowledge Counts?*. Journal of Applied Psychology. 80. 403-417. 10.1037/0021-9010.80.3.403.

3   Babcock, Linda and Lowenstein, George. (1997) *Explaining Bargaining Impasse: The role of self-serving biases. Journal of Economic Perspectives.* 11 (1) 109-126

4   Yukl, G. A. (1974). *Effects of situational variables and opponent concessions on a bargainer's perception, aspirations, and concessions.* Journal of Personality and Social Psychology, 29(2), 227–236.

5   Hilty John A. and Carnevale Peter J. (1993) *Black-Hat/White-Hat Strategy in Bilateral Negotiation* Organizational Behavior and Human Decision Processes. 55(3)., 444-469

6   Kwon, S. and Weingart , L. (2004) *Unilateral concessions from the other party: concession behavior, attributions, and negotiation judgments* Journal of Applied Psychology. 89(2). 263-278

[7] Lewicki, R. J., Barry, B., & Saunders, D. M. (2020). Negotiation (Eighth edition.). McGraw-Hill.

[8] Carr, A. (1968) *Is Business Bluffing Ethical?* Reproduced in Harvard Business Review. Accessed at https://hbr.org/1968/01/is-business-bluffing-ethical on 5 January 2023

[9] Fisher, R., Ury, W., & Patton, B. (2006). *Getting to yes* (2nd ed.). Penguin Putnam

[10] Langer. E., Blank. A. and Chanowitz. B. (1978) *The Mindlessness of Ostensibly Thoughtful Action: The role of "Placebic" information in interpersonal interaction.* Journal of Personality and Social Psychology. 36(6). 635-642 retrieved from https://jamesclear.com/wp-content/uploads/2015/03/ copy-machine-study-ellen-langer.pdf on 5 January 2023

[11] Refer Endnote 10

[12] Kahneman, D., (2011) *Thinking, fast and slow.* Farrar, Straus and Giroux.

[13] See the video at https://www.bing.com/videos/search?q=you+tube+fast+and+slow+kahneman&&view=detail&mid=25EBCF1339C71E0B7E8F25EBCF1339C71E0B7E8F&&FORM=VRDGAR for a summary of System 1 and System 2 thinking.

[14] https://www.ted.com/talks/daniel_kahneman_the_riddle_of_experience_vs_memory#t-402548

[15] In this case, the holiday was proposed just before I was leaving to go and live overseas for an extended time. In order to convince me

to come on the holiday, he pulled out the "If we don't go now, we'll never get a chance because I'll be dead before you come home." If only I'd known then what I know now!

[16] https://kilmanndiagnostics.com/overview-thomas-kilmann-conflict-mode-instrument-tki/

[17] Ury. William. *Getting to Yes With Yourself: (and Other Worthy Opponents)*. (2015) HarperOne, An Imprint of HarperCollinsPublishers,.